Reading Maps and Globes

by Ellen Bari

PEARSON
Scott Foresman

Editorial Offices: Glenview, Illinois • Parsippany, New Jersey • New York, New York
Sales Offices: Needham, Massachusetts • Duluth, Georgia • Glenview, Illinois
Coppell, Texas • Ontario, California • Mesa, Arizona

A globe is a model of our Earth. Globes are shaped like Earth and are round like a ball. People use globes to see where places are. Globes make it easy to find land, water, and oceans.

Maps are drawings that take our round Earth and put it on flat paper. You can find roads, water, countries, and cities on a map.

You can bring maps with you. Maps can be folded and are easy to carry. A book of many maps is called an atlas.

This photograph shows a park that has forests and mountains. **Mountains** are the highest kind of land. A forest is a large area with many trees and plants.

This area is home to thousands of different plants and animals. The trees and mountains make it a good place for them to live.

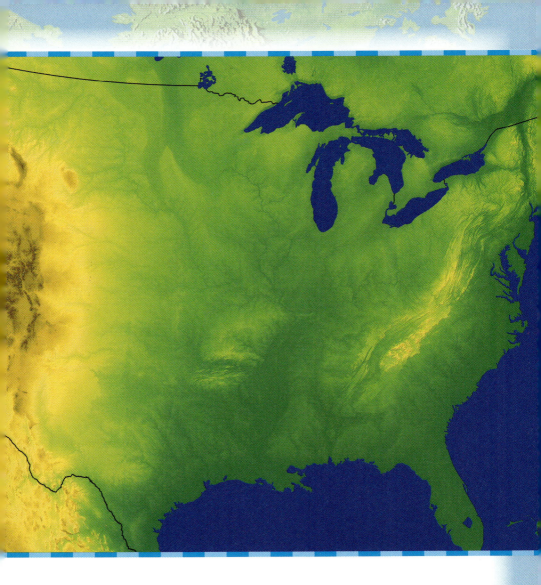

Colors can be used on a map to show what things are. Different colors mean different things. There are many green parts on this map. The green shows that there are many forests.

This is a picture of a beach. The water is the **ocean**. An ocean is a very large body of salt water. Oceans cover much of Earth.

In this photograph, it is easy to see where the shore ends and the ocean begins. The shore is the land along the ocean water.

Like maps, globes also use colors to show what things are. Blue is the color used for oceans, **rivers**, and lakes. If you look at how much blue is on the globe, you will see that there is a lot of water on our Earth. There is more water than land!

The colors on maps and globes can help you learn about your world.

Glossary

mountain the highest kind of land

ocean a very large body of salt water

river a long body of water which usually moves toward a lake or the ocean

Reading Maps and Globes

by Ellen Bari

Editorial Offices: Glenview, Illinois • Parsippany, New Jersey • New York, New York
Sales Offices: Needham, Massachusetts • Duluth, Georgia • Glenview, Illinois
Coppell, Texas • Ontario, California • Mesa, Arizona

Reading Maps and Globes

by Ellen Bari

Editorial Offices: Glenview, Illinois • Parsippany, New Jersey • New York, New York
Sales Offices: Needham, Massachusetts • Duluth, Georgia • Glenview, Illinois
Coppell, Texas • Ontario, California • Mesa, Arizona